I Was Thinking of Beauty

Also by Sydney Lea

Poetry

Six Sundays Toward a Seventh
Young of the Year
Ghost Pain
Pursuit of a Wound
To the Bone: New and Selected Poems
The Blainville Testament
Prayer for the Little City
No Sign
The Floating Candles
Searching the Drowned Man

Fiction

A Place in Mind

Essays

A North Country Life: Tales of Woodsmen, Waters, and Wildlife
A Hundred Himalayas
Hunting the Whole Way Home
A Little Wildness

I Was Thinking of Beauty

Sydney Lea

Four Way Books
Tribeca

for beautiful Robin, again and again

Please direct all inquiries to:
Editorial Office
Four Way Books
POB 535, Village Station
New York, NY 10014
www.fourwaybooks.com

Library of Congress Cataloging-in-Publication Data

Lea, Sydney, 1942-
  I was thinking of beauty / Sydney Lea.
     p. cm.
  Poems.
  ISBN 978-1-935536-31-4 (pbk. : alk. paper)
  I. Title.
  PS3562.E16I93 2013
  811'.54--dc23

                         2012029329

This book is manufactured in the United States of America
and printed on acid-free paper.

Four Way Books is a not-for-profit literary press. We are grateful for the assistance
we receive from individual donors, public arts agencies, and private foundations.

State of the Arts

NYSCA

This publication is made possible with public funds
from the New York State Council on the Arts, a state agency.

[clmp]   We are a proud member
          of the Council of Literary Magazines and Presses.

Distributed by University Press of New England
One Court Street, Lebanon, NH 03766

Contents

Metaphor

— for Stephen Arkin

The skins of maple florets have burst
and scaled to ground to sprawl
on the season's bright new shock of green.
A man out walking thinks red snow.
Each May this scene's the same
but scenery's not what he's after.
No he's come out as much for invention as air.
He's glad for what the eye can impose
even on nature less comely than this is.
The walker pauses

searching for illustration.
Ah watercolors of Venice by Turner.
Coal from old furnaces smogs their skies
so their sunsets weep and shimmer.
The paintings invite a conclusion—
Beauty will find its way.
What a mere museum-goer might call
repugnant the artist exploits.
His creations thus show a kind of transcendence.
In the middle distance

a sharpshin hawk skims the ridge of his roof
to stab a perching sparrow.
The man stops walking to watch
frail feathers hover where bird had been.
Then they're broadcast by chill spring wind.

He'd like to make something of the scarlet stream
that must trickle from peak to eaves-trough.
He compares a moment years back
amid lush islands under clouds that were doubled
in a green sea's panels

and appeared the more lovely for that.
Some predator fish had made a kill.
Stains drifted rosy by his rented rowboat.
They were lovelier still than the clouds.
Old memories too of a friend's dying words—
but after all what were they?
And why think now of their long-gone speaker?
It's not really speech he conjures:
chemotherapy had made fine dark tattoos
of vein and bruise.

Beauty will find its way.
He knows full well he should challenge that motto
as he strolls here in perfect health.
He knows his tropes make his scenery.
Metaphor is will.
Still he clings to obliging figures
like that gemlike blizzard under waking maples.
Beyond the maples there's factory smoke
which the man on his walk can't see.
At the end of their day

workmen fling steel hats into lockers.
Metal rattles and clangs on metal.
The walker hears nothing of that
but will head for home like the workers.
The splendid sun has guttered.
Real bullets savage body and bone.
Real blood stains real snow.
Somewhere. Somewhere. Somewhere.
Blood there scents the actual air.
He won't let himself smell or hear,
he won't entertain that mode of vision
for fear of meeting it here.

Peaceable Kingdom

Doesn't everyone dream of heaven?
After quarrel, he wishes his own could land at his feet.
He's on foot. As he passes the round Shaker barn on Route 7,
On an April afternoon of what's called *unseasonable heat,*
His eyes alight on two ravens, crisp contours obscured
By the asphalt's shimmer. They gorge on a flattened hare,
Winter pallor vanished but for some streaks in the clotted fur.

In heaven, he reasons, there is no loss,
No accident, everything knows its way.
The carnivores lie down with the herbivores.
It's a famous claim. By extension, no snowshoe hare ever strays
Into traffic—or if it does, it rises—and raptors
Feed on seeds, and a wife and husband never
Battle, and Pharaoh's armies all have drowned long since, each soldier

Rolling up and back in the ocean's rote,
His eyes rimed innocent white with salt.

House of Women

The last of that war is all fragment, vignette at best.
He's barely three. The house houses nothing but women.
Mother and grandmother, cousins and aunts, the husbands
in Europe or Asia, in what the women call *theater*.
      There's theater here, he believes.
But how can he know such a concept, having never seen play
nor film, and television unheard of? He crouches

in the curtained kneehole of Aunt Fay's vanity table
as she daubs on morning makeup. He parts the cloth
as if for a show—which it is—and seated so, Fay
looks lovely. She's always lovely, and it's not cosmetics
      that make her a beautiful lady.
It's her polio-withered leg that causes the lurch
when she rises, but the lurch is part of the drama, the beauty.

All done, she sighs. She kills the light and sips
a taste of something, and tells him not to tell.
He won't. She puffs at a cigarette and sighs.
Perhaps she misses the deadbeat Uncle Nick,
      who isn't that yet, the deadbeat.
He's living somewhere on a ship. The boy doesn't care.
Their daughter Nancy's fifteen, and flirts with him,

though *flirt* is another word he can't yet command.
Her kisses are simply sweets from the stores of the women.
limitless, warm. The sun stands theatrically low,

the summer lawn gone dark when the stranger appears,
        burly and strapping in khaki.
He has nerve enough to dash right up the drive
and into the house as if he owned it. The child

at the nursery window upstairs stands watch in shock,
the end of the world so near. He's sick with terror.
Meanwhile the high-heeled shoes of his frenzied mother
go avalanching downstairs despite his howls.
        The impostor lifts and swings her
round and round, till earth must seem as distant
to her as a star. His own days of stardom are over.

Dead Farms

—*Caledonia County, 2011*

Veinous snapshots of Dad Before He Went Over:
the photographs have sat on small tables so long
that the sons can't even see them. In the dark of their trailers,

from the black-and-whites the sons would have to imagine
cornsilk's yellow, roof-metal bleeding orange,
red granite gate posts, glints of mica in fieldstone.

But the sons aren't a sort to imagine. Their fathers chose—
or was it their women who chose?—each picture's background:
shed and tractor, garden, wellhead, plow.

Breeze lifts the farmers' hair; they're never indoors.
Each smokes or holds his favorite brand of smoke.
Lucky? Camel? Chesterfield? Who cares?

Say he survived tobacco and bullet and bomb;
things change, he's gone. But women as always look
to the laundry and housework. In listing mobile homes,

they make the worlds of absent men go round,
scraping up suppers that often wait in a pan
on a cooling back-burner. Among these uprooted sons

are a miserable few who madden themselves with curses
on wife or girlfriend. They went off to Viet Nam
and are wards now, field-dirt dumb, reviling their nurses.

Murder makes the odd headline. More commonly, beatings.
Was it always like this? Will it be? In their own sons' heads
will women conspire, all of them bent on cheating

male partners blind by inscrutable female cunning?
But what could be robbed from such men? Their pickups? Their dead-
end piecework jobs? Their barstools? They'd say, *Well, something—*

but they aren't a sort to say something. A world of wars
jets through their veins. In the batterers' own framed pictures,
you'll notice more often than not that they're carrying arms,

propping their feet on the chest of a kill in autumn.
It's a buck, it's never a doe, which might leave you bewildered
unless you were versed in what's left of deer camp tradition,

sad remnants their boys will inherit, while women still pour
nurture on all these farmers' heirs, who'll crave it
and hate it. Is war the appropriate metaphor?

There could be others no doubt—like seeds with surfeit
of nourishment, whose fruit can never quite sweeten.
Extravagant vines will smother, or else will turn it

so bitter it leaves the one who tastes it weeping.

You Listen to Dexter Gordon

Miss X was gentle. She helped you climb the staff,
those lines on which hung E-G-B-D-F.
Every Good Boy Does Fine, she told you, smiling,
to remind you which note went where. And perhaps to soothe you.
But there'd be more climbing, and you knew you'd never make it,
you fat little stupid oaf. You would drop piano:
two clefs were too much—you never learned the bass—
and life seemed already overcomplicated.
Kind X, goodbye. You took up with Mr. Y.
By now it wasn't the notes that exasperated,

but that you couldn't manage to make your fingers
function so the sax could soar into song.
The squawks. The broken reeds. Your breaking soul
when Y named you Shit-for-Brains, or when he claimed
he might as well be talking to a wall:
Maybe a mother could love you, but I can't stand you!
You'll admit you didn't ever practice much,
though you weren't lazy, no matter the things he yelled.
Laziness figured in less than plain awareness:
you'd never be Dexter Gordon—or much at all.

Home meant discord and drink, so Y was wrong
about mother-love, because you could have practiced
your scales and whatever else might be expected
until—cliché leaps in—you went blue in the face.
You'd be what she said you were.
A lifetime later,

Dexter whispers his way through "Don't Explain."
You want to explain nonetheless. You bring to mind
the easy trick of the easy piano teacher
for the gaps *between* the lines: *F-A-C-E*.
She said, *Your face is all you have to remember,*

then touched your cheek, which, no, no practice had blued.
You were already blue enough when you listened to Y,
or ached for some girl from what seemed unbreachable distance,
or heard the household's silences, mutters, roars.
Dexter moves on to "Guess I'll Hang My Tears
Out to Dry," and you breathe, *Every good boy does fine.*
You should have paid attention to sweet Miss X—
because weren't you good? You wanted to be at least,
though even you couldn't stand the sight in the mirror,
before you climbed into bed, of your own face.

Farmall Cub Tractor

It's really no mystery now that it felt like heaven:
Dad set the throttle, you'd circle half the day
after he left you, down and up in the saddle
with every rut and rock. The meadow lay

capacious, house to pond. The groan of the engine
muted the clatter of grasshoppers, flushed in their dozens.
You don't recall this as thrilling, because it was deeper:
delight not in the new but in an accustomed

procedure, as infants delight in nursing. A hemlock,
stunted at water's edge, was your steady marker
to turn uphill again along the brook,
gone dry by July; the constant circling vultures

above Blood Ridge looked down on your own rotations;
the road's bright gravel winked through a hedge of brush
that bordered the place to eastward—everything yours!
Forever yours. No wonder then that you pushed

the wandlike hand-throttle north a couple of notches
for speed, as your father had warned you never to do,
when Billy, chubby son of unfriendly neighbors
who lived on the hedge's far side, came waddling through,

heaved himself up, and sat on a pitted fender.
His presence alone eclipsed the hemlock, the glow
from the pond, the graceful birds. No wonder you steered
for the hummock of dirt piled tall near a woodchuck's bunker . . . .

You took it full-on. That made the left hind wheel
heave high, fat Billy lurching forward and under
the right, which pitched even higher over his mass
of body. Your blood went wintry. And yet—a wonder!—

he stood right up, red treadmarks traced on his back.
You didn't know how to stop, you'd never learned,
and the crisis seemed over. Stopping would have to wait
until Dad walked down from the house, swung on behind,

pulled the rig out of gear and thumbed the kill switch.
Those marks on Billy as he jiggled and jogged toward home
still haunt you a little, though somehow he never mentioned
that day to your parents, to his, to anyone.

You kept the secret too. But the pleasure you'd known:
the moment made it clear it was altered forever.
There's no telling where Billy may have landed since,
but your father fell dead in the meadow too shortly after.

And the meadow itself is gone, the pond dammed up
so that hucksters who sell those homes with keyhole drives
can trumpet *Lakeside Frontage!* The house is razed,
the Farmall mere scrap, if any of it survives.

The Vanishing

. . . you are like graves which are not seen, and men walk over them without knowing it.

—Luke, 11:44

We all insist ever since that we knew he'd end up a corpse.
He had no skill, or rather will, to temper whatever
he chose to say, and there was something anyway
that got on your nerves before he so much as opened his mouth.
His uncombed hair, a sort of bronze not found in nature—

even that would strike you as insult. Give him a drink
and there'd be things much worse to make you clench your teeth.
Though he came from central Europe somewhere, his English was pure,
except that he clung to and flaunted his accent. He used a *v*
for *w*, just for example, in this or that word, which seemed

a way for him to stress his status as an alien
in every sense of the term. He got into idiot fixes,
which appeared a sort of mission. Blame the booze, I'd reckon:
why else, to mention one case, insult a mammoth marine,
call him a *half-ass, chickenshit pansy?* That cost him eight stitches.

So we all disliked him. And then he disappeared completely,
never again to be seen. Of course there wasn't one
among us to insist on a search. I'd known him too well myself,
and I certainly wouldn't go to the law. He was nothing to me.
And yet that categorical vanishing lends to the wind

along our local river an eloquence after dark
it never had before. What it may be eloquent *of*
I'm not ready or able to say, nor can I tell you why
that edgy articulation should echo in the sirens
of cruiser or ambulance, of birds that cry in the night

and even ones that sing by day, like phoebe or dove.

You of the Mottoes

Near Mount Etna, it was, where ruin appeared
a thing of the past: the stelae shining
in the Latin evening, their mottoes eroded,
quick swifts breasting the sun in flight.
He ground his teeth,
                              his young mind arcing
age to age, from Vergil's Mars
to the astronauts'. He was always impatient,
always wanted more. Obscurely.
She watched harpoonists pursue a swordfish
out on the bay and breathed, *How lovely,*

and sipped her wine. Breeze tousled the blazing
gorse, and sculpted fragments waved
in her rounded eyes. A mumbling monk
swished past, head canted, as if he were hanging
on the Virgin's words.
                              Years later today.
Breeze ruffles this blanket of New England clover
and there's no one with him except his dog.
The ruin, he thinks, is now after all,
is always now, as if he had failed
to mortar one of a building's walls

for winds to topple. The bachelor won't have her
back, nor the swifts, nor the statuary
in those red-brown eyes, nor olive smoke,
nor that street musician ineptly crooning
Caro mio ben'.

He's more than weary
of the nine that one stitch might have saved,
of repeating ruin, devoid of quaintness.
He squints at a starling and mumbles, *A bird
in the hand is worth...* He sees it's true:
He's the bald rolling stone of that other proverb,

the *You* of the ancient warnings, *You*
of the mottoes—old, and now, and new.

Blind, Dumb

Ted was the logger, I the greenhorn professor,
Tommy the logger's teenaged son.

I needed distraction, so we took that hike together.
Toward evening a doe crashed past, haphazard.

Ted said, *She's blind.*

She showed as pale as a moose in the dead of winter,
which seemed foreign to me. But then everything did:

the weeks dragged by and my poor wife still lay under
the pall of coma. Our old car had flipped.

I stood and wondered,

how could the doe survive the coming cold?
The full dark loomed, and Tommy pled,

Can't we go for a gun? He didn't want to leave her
to starvation, predation, to that murder of ravens

perched low and bold.

My wife and I had quarreled. She sped away,
blanched by anger I tried to ignore

until the trooper called at the house to say
the Jeep had landed roof-down on Route 4.

On this later day,

the logger appeared to see what I couldn't see:
Not up to us to spare her, he drawled.

My every instinct wanted to disagree,
but as Tommy and I glanced up at the cruel

black birds in the trees,

I was the mute one. Dodging the frantic animal,
we could almost look through her ghostly hide,

scourged bloody by lashes of brush in her scrabbling circles.
Scavengers waited for quarry to die,

sat patient, preened.

I'd read no novel, no poetry that trained
my soul for this—or anything.

So I thought as I felt my uselessness in the scene.
What could I say? What could I do?

My vapid dream

was to start all over again, not having to know
some categorical, unspeakable things.

I'd always imagined words' restorative power,
but I'd witnessed beings who couldn't pass on

what had happened or how.

Words wouldn't help them. To see that so starkly stung.
Speechless, benighted, what had I to teach

a student now, much less a daughter or son?
Frost had unclothed the maple and ash,

so winter could come.

Art

—*for Fleda*

It seems so different   art that moves me now
From the sort of art I longed for long ago
Soaring Vatic Agon

I waited yesterday on the unsure shoulder
Of a drenched back road   From my car I could behold
Our highway agent Gordon

Fill a rut with a spade   climb up on his grader
And smooth things smooth as the top of a kitchen table
There were frost heaves by the score

And culverts clotted shut by April floods
So it was brilliant   what Gordon did with mud
On Wallace Hill   Pure mire

Out there   The road goes narrow as a needle
On which   you might wonder   could dance how many angels
I don't care   I didn't

No earthly need to summon spirits   daemons
No sign of them at all   Nor would I dream one
I might have once but wouldn't

Nor gyre nor golem   Nor great Leviathan
Nor djinn   Nor fiend   Nor signifying wind
Nor *Elementargeist*

That lingering in that lane might make me conjure
I had to get somewhere and fetch my daughter
To bring her home   Sweet Christ

She might be standing in that mix of sleet
And ugly rain   which called for Gordon's art
I'm trying to be a grownup

Better late than never   I suppose
Or am I only jaded   I don't know
It was as though I'd shown up

Just to see him wield his spade and blade out there
It kept me from surmising some *furor*
divinis   Why should I bother

Now that I moved on   thanks be to Gordon
Who signaled with his thumb for me to pass him
He pulled the grader over

Yes give me something useful here   I said
Impromptu   In my car it sounded odd
To say it now sounds different

I hope that Gordon watched me yesterday
As I signaled back   I'd never have made my way
Without a skillful agent

I hope he saw me wave

Winter Poet

Again the full moon climbs, precisely on time.
What else would it do? A shame that as it floats
it doesn't spark interior commotion.
Or perhaps it does in its way. What it produces
is no less familiar, though, than moonlight on snow.
Fireplace wood, well aged, neither cracks nor hisses
but makes a soft dull hum. He's just come to
from a doze, with someone's book of poems on his chest—
which he sets aside. He suspects if he opens it now
he'll shut it. Not that he won't find time to persist
in reading it later. He has little else to do.

He watches as shadows extend themselves on the lawn.
Also chimeras. He's tired of tired old tropes
using shadow and light. But what does he want at his age?
He's seen enough to hold to what he's got,
to the lovely, faithful, intelligent woman he owes
for what at its best is bliss, and even his cat,
who after a nap of his own seems focused upon
an angle of parlor baseboard. If he longs for his children
to be children once more, for instance, he knows they're gone
to live with their children, and all his magical thinking
will never transform them to rosy infants again.

Perhaps this is more than anything else what unnerves him:
that memory's his topic, he can't resist it
and seek out something more lively. This afternoon,
inventing a chore to cure his idle brooding,

he revised his ragged address book, which largely consisted
of rubbing out names of the lost. He'll be a witness
to more funeral ceremonies now than weddings.
Not that he'll make *memento mori* his theme,
since that's as hackneyed too as a fat moon's rising.
He hates his incapacity to behave
or express himself these days without ironizing,

to dream as he used to dream some absent lover
and how he'd been wronged by her, by the world's meanness,
the witless incomprehension of those around him
—dull, bourgeois like him now—of colorful pain.
As if that kind of thing had ever been less
a commonplace either than the dreary return of moonlight.
He still can muster the risibly easy sort
of phrasing he once thought fresh: *There you will sit,
lonely, adjusting a lamp, as I step abroad
into moonshine.* He almost sees the lover pore
over things that he could explain to her were frauds.

Abattoir Time

The widower pushed the tailgate shut and fell.
The two sounds—*click* and *thud*—seemed synchrony,
As if one in fact were function of the other.
The red calf, bound for veal in the pickup's bed,
Looked rearward over his shoulder. No one there.
A ginger-hackled rooster, framed by the door
Of the loft, screamed loudly, sun igniting him
To noontime flame. He sent six hens in a dash
For cover under bush and sill, as though
His love-assault might be a thing far worse
Than the farmer felt—or rather did not feel,

The death so quick and commotionless his livestock
Didn't notice. Everything once had purpose
Here, and meaning, and might still have, if only
He'd stayed to read them. Now a skinny cloud
Rode unremarked on a breeze above the barn,
Unsafe and leaning. His horse, a spavined relic
From other ages, whickered behind the house,
All canted too, its paint mere scattered flakes.
Meaning and purpose had blurred in recent years
But the farmer kept right after them no matter.
Who'd free the weanling now, who lead him to slaughter?

Ars Vitae

—*for Ted Leeson*

All I've said—I made it up, including the Things that Really Happened.
Outside my window now, above the autumn pond I've conjured,
two dapper kingfishers start to flit as I dream them,

and in morning fog the trees of October show brightly because just now I've imagined
a sun so sharp it could make you bleed. Once—*think of* the number!—
seven lithe otters led me and my brother

downstream as we two fished the mighty Missouri. That's a memory of Montana,
which is "not a place," as I'm reminded by a favorite western writer,
"but the name of a place." There are dogs I've treasured, quick

and lost, and horses and songs, and people, living and gone—although in fact
they're only what I've concocted from a life of talk. And yet whatever
I've talked about is fact. It must be true

or else I only had some maps, I had no place. Nor did I know
old woodsmen or their stories, to choose an example, but only read
a book or two. I had nothing. I never knew

a soul, a thing. I made up the eagle I saw today as he stooped to the neck
of a Canada goose. I made up the goose, which collapsed at the river's edge,
which I also devised. She fell close by, as dead

as if I'd shot her myself as I paddled. I intended to stop and watch that eagle,
whose tail still showed dark stripes, which means I'd made him into a young one:
I'd stop with an eye to beholding another dive

from a blighted elm that leaned at what I'd construed as just the proper angle.
But I kept on moving northward, fabricating the umber and mauve
leaves that floated upriver, counter to reason,

beside my gliding wisp of canoe. I invented the leaves so I could conceive
that backwash of eddy, and feel it move me—like many of my visions,
including those of Things that Really Happened—

as if my up were down, and my progress that fluent, easy, at least for moments.

Teacher at Cloudland Falls

Sunlit in April afternoon,
far down in the valley, ribbons of green—
first green that Frost called gold, and said
it can't stay. To reward his climb, the cascade
jets mist that's coruscant with silver.

He thinks of Eddie, son of a farmer,
and how two storeys up in a gilded mow
they wrestled together a haybale fort.
Dust motes—much like these droplets now—
flitted in angular beams of light

that poured from the barn's one roofline window
down to its buckled floorboards. Smoke
glided through the beams as well, having billowed
out the door-hole they'd left so they could peek
at invented foes. Their cigarettes

came from a pack of those weird Kool straights:
at the unlit ends, fat rings of brown
like filters—which had not yet been discovered.
Whom did they steal their contraband from?
What difference? The two boys hacked and whispered,

unaccountably joyful. Doubtless the sun's
pyrotechnics prompt these recollections.
He shivers, imagines conflagration.
How did they live out those foolhardy hours?
The teacher wonders if Eddie's grown

as responsible as he is himself these days:
he'll carry out every scrap of his waste,
paper, plastic, apple cores.
There's still some snow on the northward-facing
flank of this northern New Hampshire trail.

The cool from its surface, he thinks, is a blessing,
like that smoky spray from the waterfall.
He last saw Eddie back fifty-some years.
In that golden hayloft, they might have died.
Now the farm is as gone as those unheeding boys,

which in itself feels enough for tears.
He stands on high, the waters roar.
They might have died, but they did taste joy.
How will he teach his class tomorrow
at the venerable, ivy-garlanded college,

if he can't distinguish regret from knowledge,
accountability from sorrow?

Small Jeremiad

I killed a catbird once when I was young.
I'd still insist I didn't really mean to,
Just noticed him and flung a thoughtless stone.

I've done much worse, so why would this live on?
My cracked LP is *Mulligan Meets Getz*.
I killed a catbird once when I was young

but why, awake at dawn, should I have turned
from husky saxes intoning "That Old Feeling"
to some poor bird at whom I flung a stone?

My thought's oblique: a catbird flew to our lawn
As I chose the record, a vestigial, unusual thing,
Like the bird in my part of New England. I cast no stone,

Yet I'm sunk in lamentation: things I have done,
Ones I have left undone. There's that old feeling....
I killed a catbird once when I was young.

My life's the only life I'll ever own.
I own it all when memory wings in.
I killed a catbird once when I was young,
Just noticed him and flung a thoughtless stone.

The Gray Museum

Flat on their tapestry hawks and hounds
and a corps of horsemen showed that much flatter
for the sleeted windows. All of Manhattan
seemed a great gray museum.
Our words went blurry. It was never romance.
Or do you insist?
I thought how mountains sag into deltas

with time. From a sill outside drab pigeons
flushed into haze and were erased.
The horsemen's woven reins went slack.
In a hotel bed
later that night, even sleep turned gray:
in my dream, a train
that huffed till the station misted like glass,

in yours, you reported, fogged coastal Maine.
To me your report proved unintriguing,
I knew you'd never seen that shore.
Our breakfast eggs
looked hueless, yolkless. Attempted speech
bleared in our mouths
and the morning newspaper faded, smearing

the sodden pulp it faded into.
I haven't thought in years of that day,
so little to draw me back to then.
You wouldn't know me,

grown vivid and colorful! And you?
You've leached away.
So what, you might ask, *is bringing this on?*

But how could you ask? What would I say?

Hum and Click

The puppy softly whined in dream
—as if she heard that subtle clicking
mixed with a hum, which seemed to come
from some electric device—then she quieted.
Inertia of summer's night had settled
on him as well, soft as bed linen.
How often he'd stood at a window, shining
a flashlight outdoors, but never determined
the source of that sound, so odd and confounding.

After so many failures, he barely pulled
himself again from mattress to floor
and down the bowed-in upstairs hall
to see what little he would. The song,
to call it that, rose out of the rough,
abandoned field uphill from the house.
I need to know what it is for certain,
he thought. He might: the moon gleamed full,
and he was only 27.

In the shine, at last, miraculous:
a hen whippoorwill who picked at gravel
while the cock, in full strut with tail upthrust,
hummed and clicked a small bird's version
of immemorial courtship rites
common to all us earthly creatures.
How pretty she was, his sleeping wife....
And tomorrow, he reckoned, *I'll know forever*
something I didn't know tonight.

Succeeding owners all renovate
parts of the house, on which that evening
moon dropped softly, however bright.
He's years along in more lasting marriage.
Some of his children now have children.
He's owned just under a dozen dogs
since he heard the whine from that puppy pointer
at whippoorwills, which hereabouts
have grown so rare he'd almost surrender

years of his life just to hear one now.

Father's Blues

Sunk in my chair, I tried to doze while members
of the Branford Marsalis Quartet were aching their way
through changes: "The Blossom of Parting." So tenderly
did they suffer, however, that I'm full awake. Blue flowers
of sadness, petal-lavish, took root in the part
of my soul where dreams might have budded. They've disappeared,
though only yesterday they all were here:
three daughters, two sons, repletion of my heart.
It took my braver wife to photograph
what I know I won't be able to scrutinize
if she hangs the picture—or at least I won't do it dry-eyed.
Sidelit by sun going down, all five of them laugh
as they improvise a moment's pose together.

One night the youngest child's best friend advised her,

It's selfish, having children. If so, our will
to raise them is hardly a sign of egolessness
but instead of our natural lust to extend ourselves.
That makes my blossom of pain narcissus, I guess.
The friend's little more than a child herself, yet truth
—however partial—hid underneath her assertion.
As our children grow away they chronicle youth's
relinquishment to time. We watch them burgeon,
bloom, and when at last they bolt and scatter,
we're reminded—the way I am by this blue tune—

that our selves are no more durable than flowers.
The years will wilt them. Every change is a wound.
Like the Psalmist's tender grasses, they flourish and fade

in a day. They all were here just yesterday.

Bald Sentiment

Older children grown and gone, one daughter
Remains at home. Her potions line the rim
Of the upstairs tub: small vials containing mixtures
Of baffling application. Or so it seems
To him. Exotic teas and leaves and herbs.
He steps into the shower to wash his hair.
A grayish bar of soap will have to serve.
He doesn't object. It's vanished into air,
his hair—or rather water; it clots the drain.
Farewell, old locks, he declaims, you who have given
Not a moment's pleasure. (O adolescent pain!)
Tart pleasure harrows him as he scents his turbaned
Teenage girl, with all her creams and balms—
The sorry, baffled gladness of affection

Mixed with her father's feckless fool intention
To keep his child forever clean of harm.

The Turning

Paper birch leaves litter the meadows.
They're like cups of an imbecile design
to catch the coming season's rains.
There may be some frost in the colder hollows,
says the radio forecast. It seems we shouldn't
have reached the end of so much quite yet.
Red mushrooms match the frail efts' red.
I've meant to look up those mushrooms but haven't
in fifty years. What else has happened
to which I've paid insufficient heed?

Yet I've heeded some broader changes for ages,
so I shouldn't be daunted. The birds that scatter
ahead of winter, like small dark letters,
are strewn over clouds as white as pages.
The children return to school, some wearing
wool jackets already, and none will ever
again be so young. The corn can't get higher.
Trees in the north slope wetlands are turning,
as are trees that have been half-killed by lightning.
The stenches of cattle and barn cling harder

to clothes of farmers, the ones we've still got.
Amid all this I think of a hole
on a ragged hillside where decades ago
a house burned down. The Touch-Me-Not
muffles a nearby brooklet's mumbles

as summer surrenders to late September.
A wooden bookcase deep in that cellar
lies clutched by the roots of a dead rock maple.
That it wasn't ruined by flame is a marvel.
The books are of course long gone—I wonder,

who were the authors? who the readers?

The Picture

for my daughter Erika, on the birth of Ivy and Creston

I found it in a box I sifted through
as I cleaned my office. How clear in mind, the time
you drew it nearly thirty years ago.

From dawn to dark, a sort of dusk prevailed,
the nightbirds up all hours. I've stumbled on
signs of ruthless murder in such a day—

intinction of snow and blood. I've pictured talons.
Not knowing what I felt, still I have sensed,
without my witness, intricate change had happened.

Snow of course can offer other signs:
sweep of a grouse's wing where it flushed and flew,
the raptor's errant jabs mere blots to the side,

no blatancy of red on the cold white cover.
In any case, it was that kind of day when you held
the blue-green crayon as gently as a mother

might her child, your hand so small I could cry.
You frowned, and carefully drew three sides of a square,
and then, above, a pair of slanting lines,

to roof your house. Then swatches of sky. You glanced
sidelong at me: did I approve or not?
I knew that this was what you meant to ask.

I chuckled. Please forgive me. I stroked your cheek.
Look at you now! A mother twice at once,
in a home built plumb and true on a leafy street.

I consider these parallelograms you drew,
each with a cross inside, to form two windows,
which, you said, were there for me and you,

"For looking down the road." The road was made
of lines as well, which—*not* quite parallel—
ran right from the doorway off the edge of the page.

I clutch you tight in mind as I did so far
back down that road, your picture done for then.
I pray your babies' dreams and landscapes are

as clean and sweet as you seemed to me that day,
a perfect figure underneath those Vs
—those harmless birds, or bird-abstractions—high

above the house in their lambent blue-green sky.

To a Young Father

This riverbend must have always been lovely.
Take the one-lane iron bridge shortcut across
the town's west end and look downstream
to where the water backs up by the falls.
Boys once fished there with butterball bait
because the creamery churned by hydro
and the trout were so rich, says my ancient neighbor,
they tasted like heaven, but better. Try to
stop on the bridge if no one's coming
to see the back of the furniture mill

in upside-down detail on the river,
assuming the day is clear and still.
I've lived here and driven this road forever.
Strange therefore that I've never taken
the same advice I'm offering you.
I've lived here, but I've too often been racing
to get to work or else back home
to my wife and our younger school-age children,
the fifth and last of whom will be headed
away to college starting this autumn.

I hope I paid enough attention
to her and the others, in spite of the lawn,
the plowing, the bills, the urgent concerns

of career and upkeep. Soon she'll be gone.
Try to stop on the bridge in fall:
that is, when hardwood trees by the river
drop carmine and amber onto the surface;
or in spring, when the foliage has gotten no bigger
than any newborn infant's ear
such that the light from sky to stream

makes the world, as I've said—or at least this corner—
complete, in fact double. I'd never have dreamed
a household entirely empty of children.
It'll be the first time in some decades,
which may mean depression, and if so indifference
to the river's reflections, to leaves and shades,
but more likely—like you, if you shrug off my counsel
or even take it—it'll be through tears
that I witness each of these things, so lovely.
They must have been lovely all these years.

Impossibilities: Wild Landscape with Children

He read while his daughter dipped her toes
in autumn-chilled water—silver, slack.
Red as the literary rose,
a bug-welt glinted on her back.

His pale son stooped by their beached canoe,
arranging drift-sticks end to end,
dreaming perhaps some derring-do,
known only to him, in gravel and sand.

He felt odd fear to behold them. Today
things are better. Of course, of course they are,
though he once thought he'd given too much away
in divorce that quieted a household war.

The man saw a moose on the opposite side,
a grand bull bursting out of the waters
where it had been wading clear to the withers.
He mentioned nothing to either child,

the moose too wild somehow, the earth
below it too wild. The father looked
again from book to child, and forth
and back from the sky to the meal he cooked

on an open flame. Spruce crowded the heath,
a muskrat sculled across the bay,
a bird alit to announce the death
of summer: arctic Canada jay,

or *Gorbie Bird,* or *Whiskey-Jack.*
The clouds, as in some garish El Greco,
turned blue, then rust, then almost black.
Jealous as *cancred, cruell Malbecco,*

the boy tried to steal his sister's peach.
The man unhanded both book and pan,
lifting the girl up out of reach.
His novel's pages splayed like a fan.

What had become of everything?
The question, he knows, was run-of-the-mill.
Yet it has to this day some grip on him.
So much remains on which he can dwell:

how the bacon twisted as if in pain,
how that jay attacked their scraps of food,
how the small rain down did rain,
then the large. How meanwhile within his head

thoughts churned, impossible, obtuse.
He wished for his children: Ellington, Mahler,
Bernini, Poussin, a world of letters,
the bird, the muskrat, even the moose.

Fathomless

I remember that store, and the nasty redneck whose stink
seemed a challenge to everyone in it. The scene
is decades old, but I'm still confused that no one
took up the challenge—including me, though I liked
an occasional fight back then. The prospect of pain

meant less to me once, I guess. An aneurism
had just killed my brother, so the pain I'm talking about
was my body's. I breathed up another pain that day.
I checked the man's beat pickup; why would he want them,
those skunks knee-deep in its bed? I left the lot

still more confused, my sweet retriever shivering
on the seat beside me. The godawful smell still clung
to the dog's wet coat, and my own. There'd be no more hikes
for us that morning: rain had arrived, bone-chilling.
If you killed a skunk, why would you keep the thing?

To kill some time, I stopped at The Jackpot View.
We've always called it that. Five mountaintops bled
into mists to my east in New Hampshire. The sudden squalls
spilled leaves on the woods-floor's pall of nondescript hue.
Now he was dead. Now my brother was dead.

I can't define any God, but only this morning,
I caught a whiff of road-killed skunk and thought
I could speak of Him or Her or It as surely
as I could tell you the slightest thing concerning
the man I'm remembering now, the one who shot

or trapped or clubbed those miserable reeking creatures.
The smallest enigmas we ever encounter remain
as hard to explain as all the epical ones.
I've failed for years to fathom the death of my brother;
but it's just as hard to understand why a scene

in an old Vermont store should linger like dead-skunk odor,
which if you've lately been tainted comes back to scent you
whenever a rain blows in—or like some pains
you may have thought you'd forever gotten over,
but which at some odd prompting come back to haunt you.

Plain Fact

My barber Paul tells me that pitching a horseshoe
can take away his troubles.
But his wife of ages has not just one but two
cancers, each incurable.

So after he fixes the crackling paper collar
to my neck and gently adjusts
the chair, he speaks of his doubt: *I wonder whether*
the 'shoes will be enough.

Not this time, I judge.

Thaw

When he fetched the morning paper, he read of the would-be bomber wrestled
down by fellow travelers. A mile in the air, but nothing exploded,
the man merely scorched his own shins. Here icicles fall and bleed on the ground,
his roof-metal pings, day yawns. He yawns at a crossword: 22 Down,
Ram's Ma'am. Tired clue for *ewe,* it baffled him once, which seems hard to imagine.
He feels as though the years since then, as soon as they get here, vanish.
An expert now, he needs no pencil, taps his pen on the puzzle,

gray grainy grid on the page. Below the fold, *Hollywood Buzzes*—
with something or other. He doesn't buzz. If he used to have a life
beyond a hobby, a dog on his lap, is this one so vapid he craves
explosion? No, and he knows it. But as trees go grainy and gray as well
with something vague, neither rain nor snow, they iterate the world's
sad flatness of feature. 19 Down: *ovum-to-be.* His children
are gone, his wife in the earth, who even in older age could be ardent.

And all around him a rampancy of things lukewarm and wizened.
Maybe terror is you, he puns, the *you* that's not ram's ma'am—nor is he
ram anymore. He sluggishly seeks a synonym for *chat*
in seven letters, 16 Across. How he needs his wife to be back,
needing her ear for his desolate whispers, whimpers.
                                        The dear deaf dachsund
breathes on him from cheek to chin. It quickens him for a moment,
that heady, delusive mixture: animal heat and animal moisture.

—*in mem. HTS*

Idiot Moon

—for Marie Cope (1965-2007)

The hard-edged candor of moon in her early rising
on a night in March engenders a thought—
something says *Listen to reason.*
Advice as old as the moon.
As old and trite.

Those hundreds today didn't sob in church over reason,
but rather unreason, infernal and pointless.
Meanwhile, the incense seething,
small manchild and widower stood
brave and straight.

It is—I've measured—a hundred and sixty feet
from our house to meadow's edge downhill
where tall grass soon enough will repeat
its annual growth and be killed.
I'll estimate

how high it has risen before I scythe it down.
But that will be eye. The ear can impose
no measures. The things it takes in
don't make a song of reason.
Such song would be sweet,

but owls chuckle grimly as snow-melt uncovers rodents'
tender tunnels through last fall's stubble.
A coyote whoops for knowing
how after an iced bitter season
the deer are weak,

especially the does, whose fawn-full bellies obtrude.
No wisdom at all in an idiot moon—
white bowl of platitude:
Do as I say, and not
as I do, she prates

from her easy seat in her easy sky, and drops
random shadow all over, and if it weren't counter
to reason, I'd cast up rocks
or rattle a clip-full of bullets
at her smug fat face.

Children's choir director: she fell down dead
—and she was only 42—
and the children sang her to bed.
It makes no sense, unless
it's *because* of such fate,

because she left her sweet measures and all she loved,
that reason remains as mute as dirt.
Some are perhaps now moved
to philosophy—not I—
while animals cry,

and birds of prey.

Too Early for Grackles

I'm up alone in an August dawn.
      There's already a milky haze on the mountains
here in full summer—too early for grackles
      to covey, the way they do come autumn.
They follow the warmth that makes its way
      down south whenever it's got a mind.
But if it's only sentimental
      idiocy to ascribe some mind
to migrant birds, it's more so still
      to find motive under the imminent chill.

Mine is the mind behind such mindless
      ideas, which hardly deserve applause.
I'm here. I'm perched at a window and stare
      outside at a square of earth, that's all.
It's green, and aging. Every bird
      in that untimely swarm is fearful
and vigilant, but for a few fleet instants
      when it nods and pecks—too sadly fearful—
at whatever's left in exhausted grass:
      grasshoppers? beetles? earwigs? ants?

Men and women and birds get born
      and live and die. Still they strategize:
in whatever souls they may have they have
      some dim faith they'll always survive,
as strange and untrue a thing to believe
      as any in nature. But that's no matter.

We humans stay alert, we believe,
        holding our vigils, as if it's no matter
that the larger world keeps right on spinning
        and after us all will go on spinning.

The birds' supply of food is waning,
        but what can they fear will prey on them now?
The skunk, the snake, the rat and owl
        are back in their holes. A month ago,
there *was* that Cooper's hawk, but I shot
        above and below him to scare him off,
and did it so often that I'm convinced
        at last my persistence scared him off.
I haven't seen him in days and days.
        How rare, such success. Hot weather stays,

so it must be too early for what I've seen,
        which can bring to mind black windows' rime,
or cruel-edged icicles poised on the eaves
        above, as if each had a mind
like some grim raptor to fall on us all—
        mother and father and daughters here
who only mean to hold to this green,
        to ripened corn, to small hours here
where remnant light is bright as the birds
        are dark that darken our summer earth.

Not Like Silvio

I have had about all I can take of myself.
—S.N. Behrman

There's a rose bush outside, like the one by the kitchen
where Serena some evenings uncovered a pasta dish,
beyond exquisite.
My new wife and I would inhale its perfumes and sigh.
Not like Silvio, her husband, who'd barely touch it.

I won't play retrospection's fool
like him as he dawdled, lachrymose, in his chair,
old alleys traced
by worms along its chestnut grain now showing
patterns. Lovely. Serpentine. Complex.

We stayed near Florence in that long-gone summer . . .
Enough! as Silvio would surely not have said.
Enough! *Basta!*
In older age I tire of memory,
don't want it to be, like his, my liveliest asset,

to call it so, in what's left of my life.
I can pledge at least henceforth that I'll offer fewer
of my rote recursions—
to the limestone arch in their tiny village, for instance,
and how one day it framed my beautiful woman;

how a pair of doves, each white as flax,
sped out at me, and in their flight passed close
above her shoulders;
how a fountain winked. Enchantment. Archaic poets
would have styled the sky *empyrean*, I'd venture . . . .

To hell with habitual reminiscence.
I'm thinking right now instead of one of my sons.
He builds guitars.
Where does it come from, his preternatural deftness?
The instruments are no doubt works of art,

to his father akin to those magical paintings
by Fra Angelico we saw in San Marco,
from which we stepped out,
my love and I, into sun and other enchantment:
a small *gelateria*, where no doubt
she was magical too, and the ice cream's flavor
of lemon so true... That son himself has children.
So does one of his sisters.
Our clan's alive. No reason to elegize
the vanished infancies of sons and daughters,

though once I held all five as babies,
their warming breaths on my neck .... Why spend my strength,
why wrack my head
like Silvio, who squandered years in invocation
of his offspring's juvenescence—and in mourning his dead?

January's whiteout weather
hails the death of a year, the stocks of the rose
outside turned wan
as phantoms while—to think of things more freshly—
a different, younger year struts boldly in.

54

Unnaming

How often he has seen this butterfly,
but he looks it up today on his way
to seventy. Perhaps he needs
a hobby, however depressing the notion.
The yellowed book says the bug's named Io.
All his companions are dropping like flies. *Oh,*

damn the winter, he complains again to himself
as cold rain hammers his metal roof.
It's not a butterfly.
Colorful North American moth,
see plate 32. He does
and remembers the story of Io. Or tries.

She was, he thinks, a victim of Zeus's predation,
but there were so many he can't count them.
Rape's bad enough. Why make her
into a cow? Then Hera tied her . . .
Who on earth cares? Why look up the rest
when all its details would quickly disperse

into smidgens and shards he knows he'd never regather,
whatever he might rediscover?
All is dispersal. Childhood
best friend John has lately dropped
dead on a trail, his snowshoes a snarl;
it turns out Willie's heart was infarcted,

the marathon runner now the moldered corpse.
He knows this bitter chill of course
won't endure, yet he savors despondence—
no matter that fields are covered in bluets
and so appear to be dressed in snow,
nor that Io came back a day ago.

I Was Thinking of Beauty

—for Gregory Wolfe

I've surrendered myself to Mingus's *Tijuana Moods*
on my obsolete record machine, sitting quiet as I sat last night.
I was thinking of beauty then, how it's faced grief since the day
that somebody named it. Plato; Aquinas; the grim rock tablets
that were handed down to Moses by Yahweh, with His famous stricture
on the graven image. Last evening, I was there when some noted professor

in a campus town to southward addressed what he called, precisely,
The Issue of Beauty. Here was a person who seemed to believe
his learned jargon might help the poor because his lecture
would help put an end to the *exploitations of capitalism*—
which pays his wage at the ivied college through which he leads
the impressionable young, soon to be managers, brokers, bankers.

He was hard above all on poems, though after a brief appearance
poetry seemed to vanish. It was gone before I knew it.
The professor quoted, *Beauty is Truth, Truth Beauty*, then chuckled.
He explained that such a claim led to loathsome politics.
I'm afraid he lost me. Outside, the incandescent snow
of February sifted through the quad's tall elm trees,

hypnotic. Tonight as I sit alone and listen, the trumpet
on *Tijuana Gift Shop* lurches my heart with its syncopations.
That's the rare Clarence Shaw, who vanished one day, though Mingus heard
he was teaching hypnosis somewhere. But back again to last evening:
I got thinking of Keats composing and coughing, of Abbey Lincoln,
of Lorrain and Petrarch, of Callas and Isaac Stern. I was lost

in memory and delight, terms without doubt nostalgic.
I summoned a dead logger friend's description of cedar waxwings
on the bright mountain ash outside his door come middle autumn.
I remembered how Earl at ninety had called those verdigris birds
well-groomed little folks. Which wasn't eloquent, no,
but passion showed in the way Earl waved his work-worn hands

as he thought of beauty, which, according to our guest,
was opiate. Perhaps. And yet I went on for no reason
to consider Maori tattoos: elaborate and splendid,
Jamaicans shaping Big Oil's rusty abandoned barrels
to play on with makeshift mallets, toxic junk turning tuneful.
The poor you have always with you, said an even more famous speaker,

supreme narcotic dealer no doubt in our speaker's eyes—
eyes that must never once have paused to behold a bird,
ears that deafened themselves to the song of that bird or any.
Beauty's a drug, he insisted, from which we must wean the poor,
indeed must wean ourselves. But I was thinking of beauty
as something that will return—here's Curtis Porter's sweet horn—

outlasting our disputations. I was thinking it never had gone.

Sober

So these were the Andes, and these the fabled *chollos*,
ponies strong enough to bear his flesh
and weight accrued
       —failed suicide, guilt and tears—
ten thousand feet to that world-commanding prospect.
The guide reported that one might with luck behold
a condor. A pair had nested here for years.

The horses surefooted shale that would scare a man
as he walked, the clouds hung mountain-vast, he hoped
the rain would wait:
       he imagined on his own
that his self, which counted so little among those grand
immensities, or anywhere, might wash
downhill to the crashing *rio*, on which his bones

would ride to the cold Pacific, dissolve within it,
as he once believed they were meant by fate to do.
Yet here he sat
       a noble horse. He was well.
Sweet wind conspired with the scents of lather, leather.
Years before, rock-bottomed, he'd never have dreamed a condor,
and still he all but feared a welcoming world.

The guide called out, *Serà allà!* The bird
would be up there. He pointed at crags
as bleak and boding

as childhood terror. Gray.
The bird was not *allà*, would not be found
that day, and it came to him clear again that wonder
lay in the thought of a God, which made him say,

O I have seen that soaring after all,
because he'd known what it can be to be
poised at an edge
          more deadly than any he climbed
just then. He felt as if he'd turned much lighter
than a lump of man like him had a right to turn.
Into his mind—or out of some greater mind—

the wide-flung wings came gliding, gold as sun.

Mahayana in Vermont

My objectives this morning were vague.
As always I'd hike these hills—
a way to keep going
against the odds age deals,
a way to keep body and soul
together, and not so much thinking
as letting things steal into mind—
but I started counting

from the very first step I took.
I wore rank old boots, ill-laced,
and patchwork pants.
Around my neck hung the frayed
lanyard of a whistle I use
to summon our trio of dogs,
who capered and yelped their pleasure
at one of our walks,

and more miraculous still,
at having me for a master.
It's true in a sense
that I always count as I wander,
though it's usually the beats of a tune
(Thelonious's "Blue Monk"
a favorite) that mark my time.
These counts felt odder,

better. We scattered a brood
of grouse at step 91.
The deerflies strafed us.
At 500 a late trillium
glowed by a ledge like a lotus.
Right along the rain kept pounding.
I was mindful of all these things
but I never stopped counting.

Life was good, and more.
It was worthy of better response.
At 1000 I thought,
Enough—and counted on.
Nothing was coming to mind.
Nothing is coming again
from my hike half the day ago
with three dogs through rain

but a mystic sense of well-being
in quietly chanted numbers.
Whatever this trance,
I treasured it as a wonder
not to be wrenched into meaning,
as in *Every second counts,*
as in *You should count your blessings,*
though of those there seems no doubt.

Acknowledgments

The author would like to thank the editors of the following periodicals, in which these poems—sometimes in slightly, sometimes in considerably different versions—originally appeared:

Agni, The Atlantic Monthly, The Georgia Review, Great River Review, Green Mountains Review, The Harvard Review, The Hudson Review, The Kenyon Review, Margie, New Ohio Review, Pleiades, Ploughshares, Plume, St. Petersburg Review, Salmagundi, Shenandoah, The Southern Review, and *Upstreet.*

Sydney Lea is Poet Laureate of Vermont. This is his eleventh collection of poetry. He has also recently published a selection of literary essays, *A Hundred Himalayas* (University of Michigan Press), and a third naturalist nonfiction volume, *A North Country Life: Tales of Woodsmen, Waters, and Wildlife* (Skyhorse Publishing). In 2012 he was recognized as a Conservation Hero by *Field & Stream* magazine.